Starting Muscle Building

Step-By-Step Guide On Body Building For Beginners With Body Building Meal Plans, Muscle Building Workouts And Body Building Tips So You Don't Over-Work Your Muscles

By:

Jake R. Martin

Copyright©. All Rights Reserved

Bodybuilding is the process of developing muscle fibers through various techniques. It is achieved through muscle conditioning, weight training, increased calorie intake, and resting your body as it repairs and heals itself before restarting your workout routine.

The workouts involved are designed to focus on specific muscle categories or groups. Foods are consumed with the intention to build the body's metabolism and increase overall mass.

Muscle building also focuses on form performing the movements with the appropriate muscle groups and not transferring the weight to different body parts in order to move great weight. If you don't use good form, you risk muscle injury, which could hinder your overall progress.

If you are a beginner at body building, you should not just "jump right in". You need to build up your strength because over-working your muscles can result to more harm than good.

Some of your muscles might be naturally stronger than others. Building up slowly allows muscles to develop appropriate strengths relative to each other.

The routines featured within this book will help you develop a solid workout quickly and easily. We will break down each of the common workout positions and exercises so that you can fully understand how they are done, as well as the muscle group they target.

Disclaimer And Terms Of Use Agreement

This information is not presented by a medical practitioner and is for educational and informational purposes only. The content is not intended to be a substitute for professional medical advice, diagnosis, or treatment. Always seek the advice of your physician or other qualified health care provider with any questions you may have regarding a medical condition. Never disregard professional medical advice or delay in seeking it because of something you have read or heard.

The author and publisher make no representation or warranties with respect to the accuracy, applicability, fitness, or completeness of the contents of this book. The information contained in this book is strictly for educational purposes. Therefore, if you wish to apply ideas contained in this book, you are taking full responsibility for your actions.

Every effort has been made to accurately represent this product and its potential. However, there is no guarantee that you will improve in any way using the techniques and ideas in these materials. Examples in these materials are not to be interpreted as a promise or guarantee of anything. Self-help and improvement potential is entirely dependent on the person using our product, ideas and techniques.

Many factors will be important in determining your actual results and no guarantees are made that you will achieve results similar to ours or anybody else's, in fact no guarantees are made that you will achieve any results from our ideas and techniques in our material.

The author and publisher disclaim any warranties (express or implied), merchantability, or fitness for any particular purpose. The author and publisher shall in no event be held liable to any party for any direct, indirect, punitive, special, incidental or other consequential damages arising directly or indirectly from any use of this material, which is provided "as is," and without warranties.

Table of Contents

Disclaimer And Terms Of Use Agreement	3
Introduction	6
Chapter 1: Training Exercises	9
Chapter 2: Extensive Workouts	22
Sample 3-Day Workout	28
Chapter 3: Power Foods Defined	32
Chapter 4: Meal Plans: Print Out	48
Sample Meal Plans	52
Cooking For Mass	57
Chapter 5: Rested Performance	76
Chapter 6: The Truth About Supplements	79
Chapter 7: Body Building For Women	90
Chapter 8: A Note About Competitions	94
Conclusion	104

Introduction

Bodybuilding is the process of developing muscle fibers through various techniques. It is achieved through muscle conditioning, weight training, increased calorie intake, and resting your body as it repairs and heals itself, before restarting your workout routine.

Workouts are designed to focus on specific muscle categories or groups, and foods are consumed with the intention to build the body's metabolism and increase overall mass.

This book will focus on weight training for body builders. Weight training develops both strength as well as the size of skeletal muscles.

It uses the force of gravity to oppose the force generated by muscles through contraction. Weight training uses a variety of specialized equipment designed to target specific muscle groups and movements.

Some people refer to weight training as strength training. While they are not exactly the same, they are both similar to each other.

Strength training focuses on increasing muscular strength and size. Weight training is one type of strength training using weights as the primary force to build muscle mass.

The basic principles of weight training are pretty much the same as those of strength training. It involves a manipulation of the numbers of reps, sets, tempo, exercise types, and weight moved to cause desired increases in strength, endurance, size, or shape.

The specific combination of reps, sets, exercises, and weight depends upon the desires of the body builder. Sets with fewer reps can be performed with heavier weights but have a reduced impact on endurance.

Equipment used in weight training includes barbells, dumbbells, pulleys, and stacks in the form of weight machines or the body's own weight as in push-ups and chin-ups. Different weights will give different types of resistance.

Weight training also focuses on form performing the movements with the appropriate muscle groups and not transferring the weight to different body parts in order to move great weight. If you don't use good form in weight training, you risk muscle injury, which could hinder your overall progress.

Another form of weight training is resistance training. Resistance training involves the use of elastic or hydraulic resistance to contraction rather than gravity. When your muscles are resisting a weight, the overall tone of that muscle will grow over time.

If you are a beginner at weight training, you should not just "jump right in". You need to build up your strength and over-working your muscles can cause more harm than good. Some of your muscles might be naturally stronger than others. Building up slowly allows muscles to develop appropriate strengths relative to each other.

Most gyms offer the services of a personal trainer that comes with the membership fee. These trainers can suggest specific workouts for you to begin with, however the routines featured within this guide will help you develop a solid workout quickly and easily.

In the next chapter, I will break down each of the common workout positions and exercises so that you can fully understand how they are done, as well as the muscle group they target.

Chapter 1: Training Exercises

Let's take a look at just some of the most common exercises and routines so you better understand the different techniques used within weight training and overall fitness.

Here are a few of the more common ones:

Dumbbell Bench Press

Sit on the edge of a flat bench with the dumbbells resting on your knees. In one smooth motion, roll onto your back and bring the dumbbells up to a position slightly outside and above your shoulders. Your palms should be facing forwards.

Bend your elbows at a ninety-degree angle with your upper arms parallel to the ground. Press the weights up over your chest in a triangular motion until they meet above the centerline of your body. As you lift, concentrate on keeping the weights balanced and under control. Follow the same path downward.

Standing Military Press

For this exercise, you will use a barbell. Stand with your legs about shoulder width apart and lift the barbell to your chest. Lock your legs and hips and keep your elbows in slightly under the bar. Press the bar to arm's length over your head. Lower the bell to your upper chest or your chin depending on which is more comfortable for you.

This exercise can also be performed with dumbbells or seated on a weight bench.

Lying Tricep Push

Sit on a flat bench holding a curl bar with an overhand grip. Lie back so that the top of your head is even with the end of the weight bench. As you are lying back, extend your arms over your head so that the bar is directly over your eyes.

Keep your elbows tight and your upper arms stationary throughout the exercise.

The biggest key to this exercise is keeping your upper arms in a fixed position.

Slowly lower the bar until it almost touches your forehead. Press the bar back up in a slow, sweeping arc-like motion. At the finish, lock your elbows completely.

Side Lateral Dumbbell Raise

Stand upright with your feet shoulder width apart and your arms at your side. Hold a dumbbell in each hand with your palms turned toward your body.

Keep your arms straight and lift the weights out and up to the sides until they are slightly higher than shoulder level.

Then slowly lower them back down to your side again.

Keep your palms turned downward as you lift the dumbbells so that your shoulders rather than your biceps do the work.

Make sure you are lifting the dumbbells up rather than swinging them up. Don't lean forward while doing this either or you risk injury to your back.

Preacher Curls

This exercise is best done with a special preacher curl bench, but you can do this without it with a little modification.

Sit at the end of the weight bench, and place something such as a firm pillow or a few pillows under your armpits on your lap. Hold the curl bar in your hands with palms facing upward.

Don't hunch over the pillow, sit as straight as you can.

Using a shoulder width grip, grasp the bar in both hands. Curl the bar upward in an arc. Be careful not to swing or rock to get the bar moving. You need to be using your muscles to lift the weight, not momentum. The goal of this exercise is to work the biceps.

Bring the bar up to your chin keeping in mind that the resistance is greatest during the beginning of the lift. Lower the bar slowly working the muscle on the way down as well.

You can also do this with dumbbells or work one arm at a time.

Seated Dumbbell Curl

Sit at the end of a bench with your feet firmly on the floor. Keep your back straight and your head up. Start with the dumbbells at arm's length with your palms facing in. Curl the weight up and twist your wrist once they pass your thighs.

Squeeze your biceps at the top and then slowly lower the weight.

Do not swing the dumbbells down; lower them as you are working those muscles! You can do this standing, but the seated position prevents bad form.

One-Arm Dumbbell Row

Start with your right foot flat on the floor and your left knee resting on a flat bench.

Lean forward so that you're supporting the weight of your upper body with your left arm on the bench. Your back should be flat and almost parallel with the floor.

Reach down and pick up a dumbbell with your right hand. Your left arm should be locked at the elbow so it will support the weight of your upper body.

Before starting, look straight ahead instead of at the floor so you can keep your back straight. Tighten your abs to keep your body from turning to the side as you lift the dumbbell.

Concentrate on pulling your elbow back as far as it can go. The dumbbell should end up roughly parallel with your torso.

After you've rowed the dumbbell up as far as you can slowly lower it back to the starting position. Switch arms after one set.

Dumbbell Shrugs

Stand straight up with your feet at shoulder width. Hold two dumbbells with your arms hanging at your sides.

Droop your shoulders down as far as possible. Raise your shoulders up as far as you can go then slowly return to the starting position.

You can also rotate your shoulders by going up in a circular motion from front to back and then back down again. This can also be done holding a barbell.

Standing Calf Raises

This can be done with a specific machine found in a gym, or adapted for use without the machine. Stand up against a wall with your body facing the wall and your palms down on the wall and your feet flat on the floor.

Keep your body straight and slowly lift up your heels until you are standing on the tips of your toes. Hold the contraction briefly then slowly return to the starting position with your feet flat on the floor.

Crunches

Lie flat on your back with your feet flat on the ground, or resting on a bench with your knees bent at a 90 degree angle. If you are resting your feet on a bench, place them three to four inches apart and point your toes inward so they touch.

Place your hands lightly on either side of your head keeping your elbows in. Don't lock your fingers behind your head! Push the small of your back down in the floor to isolate your abdominal muscles. Begin to roll your shoulders off the floor.

Continue to push down as hard as you can with your lower back.

Your shoulders should come up off the floor only about four inches, and your lower back should remain on the floor. Focus on slow, controlled movement - don't cheat yourself by using momentum!

Dumbbell Hammer Curls

With a dumbbell in each hand, stand with your arms hanging at your sides, and palms are facing each other. Keep your elbows locked into your sides. Your upper body and elbows should remain in the same place during the whole lift.

Keep your palms facing each other, curl the weight in your right hand up in a semi-circle toward your right shoulder. Squeeze the biceps hard at the top of the lift and then slowly lower.

Do not turn your wrists during this lift! You can also do one arm at a time and/or alternate.

Incline Dumbbell Press

Sit on the edge of an incline bench set at about a 45-degree angle. Pick up a dumbbell in each hand and place them on your thighs.

Then, one at a time, raise them up to your shoulder level while you press your back and shoulders firmly against the bench.

Press the weights back up to a point over your upper chest, with your palms facing forward. Lower the weights slowly. Inhale as you lower the weights and exhale as you lift.

Barbell Squat

Rest a barbell on the upper portion of your back, not your neck. Firmly grip the bar with your hands almost twice your shoulder width apart.

Position your feet about shoulder width apart and your toes should be pointing just a little outward with your knees in the same direction.

Keep your back as straight as possible and your chin up, bend your knees and slowly lower your hips straight down until your thighs are parallel to the floor. Once you reach the bottom position, press the weight up back to the starting position.

Don't lean over or curve your back forward! You can use a belt to help reduce the chance of lower back injury. You can put your heels on a 1 inch block to further work the quads. You can also use a wider stance to work the inner quads even more.

Upright Barbell Row

Stand upright and grasp a barbell with your hands about shoulder width apart. Let the bar hang straight down in front of you. Keep your body and wrists straight. Pull the bar straight up towards your chin, keeping it close to your body.

Concentrate on either pulling with your traps or the front of your shoulders, depending on what you want to work most. Lower slowly to the starting position. Don't cheat by leaning forward or backward. Don't swing!

Front Dumbbell Raise

Stand with a dumbbell in each hand, palms facing backward. Your feet should be about shoulder width apart. Maintain a slight bend in your elbows throughout the exercise so that your arms are straight, but not quite locked.

Lift the weight in your left hand in front of you in a wide arc until it is slightly higher than shoulder height.

With a smooth, controlled motion, lower the weight while simultaneously lifting the weight in your right hand, so that both arms are in motion at the same time.

Do not cheat by swinging or leaning backwards! This lift can also be done with two dumbbells at the same time or a barbell.

Stiff Leg Barbell

Place a barbell on your shoulders. Keep your head up and your back completely straight.

Bend at your waist with your legs locked, until your upper body is parallel to the floor.

Return slowly to the upper position. This can also be done with your knees slightly bent.

One Leg Barbell Squat

Use a 12 to 18 inch box or bench for this exercise - the higher the box, the more difficult the exercise. Place a barbell behind your head at the base of your neck. Grasp the barbell with both hands with a wider than shoulder width grip.

Stand approximately 2 to 3 feet from the box and turn so that the box is directly behind you. Reach one foot back and place your toe on the box.

Keep your opposite foot flat on the floor and point your toes forward. Stand up straight. Keep your back tight and your chest out throughout the entire exercise.

Keep your head and neck in line with your torso so that you are looking forward. Your shoulders should be directly over your front foot.

Keeping your front foot flat on the floor, sit your hips back (like you are going to sit in a chair), bend your knee (of your front leg), and lean forward slightly at the waist.

Lower your body in a controlled fashion until your thigh (of your front leg) is parallel to the ground.

If you have difficulty lowering yourself down this far, lower yourself until the knee of your front leg is bent 90 degrees.

At this point, your knee should be directly over your toe, your hips should be sitting back, and your chest should be directly over the middle of your thigh.

Now, leading with your head and chest, raise yourself by pushing your hips slightly forward and up toward the ceiling, and straightening your leg. Return to the starting position.

At this point, your shoulders should be directly over front foot.

Lunges

Place a barbell on your upper back. Lift your chest up and look straight ahead. Position your right leg forward in a long stride.

Your foot should be far enough in front of you so that when you bend your right knee, your thigh and lower leg form a right angle.

Slowly bend your knees, lowering your hips so your rear knee just clears the floor. Pause briefly in this position, then slowly straighten your legs and raise your body back up to a standing position.

Complete a full set, then switch legs and repeat, or alternate legs for each rep.

Make sure your knee does not travel past your toes in the down position! This can also be done with dumbbells in each hand instead of using a barbell.

Barbell Tricep Extension

Hold a barbell with hands a little closer together than shoulder width. Lie on an incline bench and position your head at the top.

Press bar overhead to arm's length. Lower the bar in a semicircular motion behind your head until your forearms touch your biceps.

Keep your upper arms close to your head. Return to the starting position. This can also be done with straight bar, 2 dumbbells, seated or standing or with 2 dumbbells and your palms facing in.

The exercises listed above can be done either in a gym or in your home. If you are going to join a gym, they will have many specialty machines that will work specific parts of your body.

Employees at the gym can help you with proper use of the machines. If you are unsure how to complete a specific exercise, make sure to ask for help so that you are maximizing your routine and following each position accurately.

Chapter 2: Extensive Workouts

Beginning a body building workout plan requires a level of commitment. As a beginner, you can work out more frequently than more advanced body builders.

The reason is simple: as you get more experienced, you learn to push your muscles harder and inflict more damage that takes longer to recover from.

Beginners, on the other hand, get sore but bounce back quicker since the muscular damage isn't as severe.

If the word "damage" makes you flinch, don't worry.

It's a good thing for a bodybuilder to incur limited muscle damage, because it nudges the body to recover and overcompensate (grow) slightly to prepare for future workouts. This is what bodybuilding is all about - a continuous cycle of one-step-back, two-steps-forward, repeated over and over on a weekly basis.

The following workout plan is designed to focus on one part of your body each day of your workout with mid week and the weekend as your rest days.

This plan is just a suggestion. You can adapt it as needed to suit your workout goals.

With any workout, you need to start out with some warm up exercises. This can be simple stretching as you get your body ready to work. A warm-up session prior to working out can not only help get your body ready for exercise, but your mind will get prepared as well.

You should also have an appropriate cool down period after you are done working out.

This will reduce the possibility of delayed muscle soreness and will help quell the adrenaline that has been building in your system as a result of the workout. This can also be simple stretching exercises and deep breathing.

Again, it's important to start out slow and not push yourself beyond your limits.

Use weights that are not too heavy for you but that will give you enough resistance to build your muscles.

You can progressively increase the amount of weight you lift as you get stronger.

Day 1 – Upper Body

For the following exercises, begin with two sets of 10-12 reps each.

Dumbbell press

Standing barbell military press

Lying tricep press

Side lateral raise

Preacher curls

Seated dumbbell curl

Dumbbell rows

Dumbbell shrugs

If you have access to weight machines, add the following to your plan:

Pec deck butterflys

V-bar pushdowns

Lat pulls with pulley machine

Day 2 – Lower Body and Abs

Again, begin doing each exercise with two sets of 10-12 reps each except for the crunches which you can do as many of them as you want.

Barbell squat

One leg barbell squat

Lunges

Standing calf press

Stiff leg barbell

Crunches

Machines can be especially helpful when working your lower body. Here are some you should consider on this day:

Leg presses on a plate loaded machine

Leg extension machine

Seated hamstring curls

Standing hamstring curls

Ab machine

Day 3 – Rest

Day 4 – Upper Body

Increase your sets to 3 doing 10 – 12 reps each

Chin ups (get assistance if necessary)

Seated dumbbell hammer curls

Dumbbell presses on an inclined bench

Standing barbell military press

Standing bicep curls

Barbell tricep extension

Upright barbell row

Front dumbbell raise

The machines you can use on this day include:

Seated cable rows

Upright cable rows

Cable crossover flies

Tricep rope pushdowns

Day 5 – Lower Body and Abs

Go back to doing just two sets of 10-12 reps each except for the crunches which you can do unlimited amounts of.

Standing calf press

Lunges

Barbell squat

Stiff leg barbell

Standing calf raises

Crunches

Machine exercises include:

Leg presses on a plate loaded machine

Seated hamstring curls

Kneeling hamstring curls

Weekend – Rest

If a four day workout plan is too much for you, consider starting out with a two or three day plan. Keep in mind that you won't get results as quickly with a fewer day workout, but if you need to start out slowly, it can still be effective.

Sample 3-Day Workout

Day 1 – Back, Chest, and Abs

Do three sets of 12-15 reps each.

Bent over barbell row

Stiff legged barbell dead lift

Barbell bench press

Incline dumbbell press

Dumbbell flies

Crunches

Day 2 – Legs and Shoulders

Do three sets of 12-15 reps each.

Barbell squat

Seated calf raise

Front dumbbell raise

Side lateral raise

Upright barbell row

Lunges

Barbell squats

Day 3 – Biceps, Triceps, and Abs

Do three sets of 12-15 reps each

Barbell curl

Incline dumbbell curl

Lying triceps press

Barbell tricep extension

Front dumbbell raise

Dumbbell hammer curls

Crunches

About an hour before your workout, you should eat some protein and carbohydrates.

This is to make sure that you have enough energy to make it through your entire workout.

By doing this, you are putting your body into an anabolic state that will provide the necessary energy and power to effectively work your muscles.

During training, there is increased blood flow to the muscles. When you consume protein and carbohydrates prior to a workout, your body can take advantage of that extra blood flow and work the muscles more efficiently.

Many people opt for a protein shake and a bowl of rice, but you can choose whatever foods you want to get what you need.

It's a good idea to keep track of your workouts and how many sets and reps you are doing.

Write it down in a small notebook and when you are able to increase the number of sets and/or reps, be sure to take note of how long it took you to get to that point.

Also keep track of the amount of weight you are able to lift and when you are able to increase that weight.

It's also a good idea to do your first set with very little weight. This is to get the blood flowing through the muscles. On the second set, add a little weight and do the exercise again. If you find that it's just a bit too easy, try more weight.

The goal is to add weight until it's difficult to complete 8-12 reps.

Remember, you want to build your body, not lift weights.

Be sure and rest between sets to allow your body to adjust and recover. Usually that's around a minute or two.

DO NOT rest more than a minute or so or else your muscles will get cold and all your previous work will be for nothing. The idea is to keep the burn, taking only very short breaks in between sets.

It's a good idea to sprinkle your workouts with some cardio exercises to help get your blood pumping. This could be a little time on a treadmill or walking. The cardio is good for your body and you'll be focusing on that most important muscle of all – your heart!

Chapter 3: Power Foods Defined

When you decide you want to undertake a body building program, the foods you eat can make a huge difference in the effectiveness of your program.

Many people don't pay enough attention to the types of food they eat. But food is very important in a body-building program.

Food supplies us with calories. Calories are tiny bits of energy that your body uses to perform work. Counting calories isn't as important as knowing what calories will be the best ones to consume for the maximum effect on your workout.

To have enough energy to perform your workout, you'll need a lot of different nutrients. One of the most important would be carbohydrates.

Carbs

Carbohydrates are the body's main source of glucose. Glucose is a simple carb that is stored in your muscles and liver as glycogen.

Glycogen is the principal form of energy that is stored in muscles. When your muscles are filled with glycogen, they both look and feel full.

Glucose

Glucose also provides energy for your brain and making blood in your body.

Glucose can be made from protein, but that requires the breakdown of body protein from muscle. If you're not eating enough carbohydrates, your body will start breaking down muscle tissue for glucose.

Carbs

Carbohydrates should be the bulk of your daily caloric intake when you are starting a body-building program.

Focus on unprocessed complex carbs like sweet potatoes, potatoes, whole grain breads, oatmeal, and brown rice.

These natural complex carbs are made of long "chains" of sugar and are digested very slowly.

Slow burning carbs promote consistent blood sugar levels, which help to offset fatigue while promoting the release of insulin, which is the body's principal anabolic hormone.

For men, the amount of carbs that should be taken in by multiplying their body weight by three. That number will be the amount of grams that should be consumed daily.

Women multiply their body weight by two to get their carb gram intake.

For example, a 200-pound man should consume 600 grams of carbs per day and a 125 pound woman would eat 250 carb grams daily.

Fiber

Along with carbs, you must consume enough fiber in your diet. Eating fiber makes muscle tissue more responsive to anabolism by improving sugar and amino acid uptake, and aiding in muscle glycogen formation and growth.

Beans and oatmeal are two excellent sources of fiber.

Divide your carb meals into six servings throughout the day. This divide and conquer approach stimulates a steady release of insulin to create an anabolic, or muscle building, state.

If you eat too many carbs in one sitting, the net effect is that fat-storing enzymes kick into high hear and you lose than lean and hard look.

Eat some simple carbs after your workout and eat more of them. Honey, sugar and refined foods such as white bread and white rice - typical simple carbs - are digested quickly and easily. The resulting insulin spike is a double-edged sword, however.

After training, it can prevent muscle catabolism while promoting anabolism. If you have not been working out, the intake of simple carbs can stimulate fat storage.

A high carb intake at your post training meal will have less chance of being stored as fat, as carbs must replenish depleted glycogen levels before they gain the ability to stimulate fat storage. Eat about 25% of your daily carbs at this meal.

Breakfast is definitely the most important meal of the day, and besides your post-workout meal, it is also the best time to load up on carbs.

Blood sugar and muscle glycogen levels are low from your overnight fast. Your body must replenish these levels before stimulating the fat storing machinery in the body.

As your day wears on, your carb intake should decrease. Your energy requirements will also decrease at this time, so your body won't need as much.

If you eat carbs late in the day, your body will store them as fat and increase weight gain instead of muscle mass.

If you feel that you need to lose fat along with building your muscles, you will want to rotate your carb intake. Bodybuilders who rotate their carb intake tend to lose more fat than bodybuilders who maintain a steady flow of carbs while dieting.

For example, instead of eating 600g of carbs every day (the typical daily total for a 200 pound bodybuilder), try varying the volume of intake.

Eat 50% fewer carbs (300g) for two days, then the standard 600g for the next two days, then 50% more (900g) for the next two days.

The total carb intake is the same, but this schedule works because it lowers muscle glycogen in the first stage (promoting fat loss), and then increases insulin levels (ensuring no loss of muscle) on the final two days. Carb rotation gives you the best of both worlds: decreased fat with no loss of muscle.

Protein

Another important nutrient every body builder needs is plenty of protein. Amino acids are the building blocks of protein. Glucose molecules make up carbohydrates just like amino acids make up proteins.

Protein is involved in growing, repairing, and replacing tissues. That is made possible because proteins are the basis for body structures.

For body builders, nitrogen balance is an important concept to keep in mind when talking about proteins.

Nitrogen balance is the difference between the amount of nitrogen taken in and the amount excreted or lost.

If you lose more nitrogen than you consume, your body will break down muscle tissue to get it. On the other hand, if you consume more than you lose, you will be in an anabolic, or muscle building, state.

Protein intake exceeds output, and protein is retained in tissue as new muscle is added. Obviously, this is something that you want.

Watch out, if your protein output exceeds intake you would have a negative nitrogen balance. This is not good because the opposite is now happening.

Your body is degrading muscle and other body proteins. You usually see this in people who are starving, burned, injured, or have a fever. This puts your body in what is called a catabolic state.

An anabolic state is when your body has a positive nitrogen balance. The term catabolic refers to the state of the body in which body compounds are broken down for energy purposes.

In body building contexts, catabolic means muscle loss. Ultimately, your body won't grow when it is in a catabolic state. The general rule is to consume daily the same amount of grams in protein as your body weight. A 200 pound body builder, therefore, would need to eat 200 grams of protein every day to put the body in an anabolic state.

When calculating the amount of protein you are eating, concentrate on the complete sources of protein like meat, fish, and eggs. While there are proteins in other foods, you need to focus on the complete sources rather than those that are incomplete.

If you are dieting while body building, your protein intake should increase to 1 ½ times your bodyweight.

Many diets have you cutting back on fat and carbohydrate intake. This forces the body to burn more protein for fuel, which can put your muscle tissue at risk. To compensate, you'll need to eat more protein to counteract this effect.

Here's a quick guide to the protein content of some common foods:

Protein-containing foods	Protein (in grams)
5 oz. steak, cooked	35
5 oz. roasted chicken	43
5 oz. tuna	43
1 egg	6
1 c. milk	8
2 T. peanut butter	9
2 slices of cheese	14
2 slices of whole wheat bread	5
1 c. cooked broccoli	5
1 c. beans (legumes)	15

Some people don't feel that loading up on protein is a good idea for anyone, but if you want to get ripped with your body building program, you'll need the amino acids in protein to work in your body.

Be aware of the amount of protein you are eating and make them work for you instead of against you.

Fats

Yes, even when you are building the perfect body, you'll still need some fats in your diet. Fats are the main source of energy in the body.

Fat combines with glucose for energy in order to spare the breakdown of protein. That way, protein can do what it is supposed to do – build muscle.

The key to fat intake is to stay away from bad fats and only eat the good fat. Saturated fat is bad.

These are the fats that contribute to heart disease and high cholesterol. Because of the chemical composition of saturated fat, your body cannot break it down very well.

Saturated fats are commonly found in animal products such as meat, seafood, whole milk dairy products like milk and cheese, as well as egg yolks.

Saturated fats elevate blood cholesterol by increasing both the good HDL and the bad LDL. Elevated levels of LDL can clog arteries and cause heart disease. They are also more readily stored as body fat, so they should be limited.

Trans fats should also be avoided. This type of fat is often used in commercially processed food because they are preserved longer. Trans fats cause an over activity in the immune system and are linked to stroke, heart disease, and diabetes. You should truly strive to eliminate all trans fats from your diet.

Unsaturated fats are easier for your body to break down. Some of them can act as antioxidants that can actually help in losing stored fatty tissue in the body. These fats are found naturally in foods like nuts and avocados. These fats have a great effect on the cardio system as they work to lower the bad LDL cholesterol in the body.

The easiest way to tell the difference between saturated and unsaturated fats is to look at them. At room temperature, saturated fats are hard and solid. Unsaturated fats are in liquid form as in oils.

So basically, you should stay away from fats like animal lard and use oils such as olive oil or canola oil. Pay close attention to the fat content of any processed foods you are eating and keep it to a minimum or else your body will store that fat as, well, fat.

Probably the best type of fat to have in your diet would be Omega 3 Fatty Acids. These fats are most often found in fish and can have some significant health advantages. They can reduce inflammation, help prevent cancer growth, and improve brain function.

Omega 3 Fatty Acids can actually help combat conditions such as depression, fatigue, joint pain, and even Type 2 diabetes. Because they reduce inflammation in the body, they are good for the body builder because they help promote muscle recovery, which can be important in the body building process.

Fats are actually an important part of any diet. They play an important role in protecting the body's vital organs. Fats keep the body insulated; maintain healthy hair and skin as well as providing a sense of fullness after meals.

Obtaining sufficient fat in its healthy form is one of the keys to good health and well-being and a great body! However, you must be careful not to overdo on the fats, so consider the following suggestions for keeping your fat intake at a healthy level:

- Snack on peanuts instead of chips or candy. About a ½ cup is a good amount.

- Use olive oil in salad dressings and when cooking

- When baking, instead of topping with chocolate or candies, consider using nuts and seeds instead

- Try making sandwiches with avocado and tuna instead of higher fat lunchmeats

- Eat fish at least three times a week to increase your Omega 3 intake

- Limit or even eliminate fast food as well as sources of trans fats like commercially processed cookies and cakes

When you start on a body building program, you will want to pay close attention to the foods you are feeding your body. That includes alcohol as well.

Many people like a drink or two or even three to help them unwind and relax. But when you are a body builder, alcohol can have a detrimental effect on your progress.

Alcohol contains nothing but empty calories. It has no nutritional value but it does contain high caloric content. In fact, just one shot of vodka contains 100 calories! Not only will drinking increase your caloric intake, it slows down your metabolism hindering your body's ability to process foods.

Alcohol consumption also hurts muscle growth. Not only will having a hangover lower your workout intensity, but drinking actually lowers protein synthesis by twenty percent. There are several reasons why it does this.

For one, it dehydrates your muscle cells. As many know, hydrated and even over hydrated muscles allows for a much higher anabolic environment. Because your cells aren't holding as much water, it becomes much harder to build muscle.

The second reason why alcohol can severely hurt muscle growth is because it blocks the absorption of many important nutrients that are key to muscle contraction, relaxation and growth including calcium, phosphorus, magnesium, iron and potassium. Not only that, but alcohol lowers the amount of testosterone in your body and actually increases estrogen levels. Having higher levels of testosterone can help with your workouts by making you more aggressive, so when those levels are down, you will not be as intense in your lifting and weight training.

Probably one of the best things you can do to help your body building workout progress the way you want it to is to drink plenty of water. Water is good for you anyway, but for body builders, it can be especially important. Water is part of every single metabolic process that the body undertakes. Most experts recommend everyone drink six to eight glasses of water daily to stay healthy. For body builders, you'll need much more. Soda, coffee, and tea don't count either. The caffeine can increase fluid loss, so you're not getting the hydration you need. Body builders need at least a half gallon to a gallon per day depending on the intensity of your workouts.

Water flushes out toxins and other metabolic waste products from the body.

Water is especially important when following a "high protein" diet, as it helps remove excess nitrogen, urea (a toxic substance), and ketones. If you're eating big to gain weight, then you need even more water to help your kidneys do their work.

Without enough water, the kidneys can't function properly. When this happens, some of the load is transferred to the liver. The liver metabolizes stored fat for energy. If the liver is doing some of the kidneys' work, it burns less fat. In addition, water can actually reduce feelings of hunger.

Contrary to popular belief, drinking water can actually help you shed excess water weight. When water is in short supply, the body, thinking there's a shortage, begins hoarding it. This water is stored in extra cellular spaces. In other words, your skin starts looking soft and swollen.

If you're going to be using supplements in your body building program, and you should, water can help them work. Supplements like creatine work in part because it pulls water in muscle cells, creating an anabolic environment needed for muscle growth. For this to work properly, you need plenty of water. Plus, if you're training hard, then you need a basic megavitamin. Many vitamins are water soluble, and water unlocks the power of those vitamins.

A good diet is essential to an effective body building program. You can workout with the intensity of a professional, but if your diet stinks, you won't be doing yourself any good.

Consider the following general tips for your nutritional needs.

- Drink skim milk or soy milk

- Cut sugar from your diet. Use artificial sweeteners instead.

- No regular soda! Diet is better for you anyway and doesn't contain sugar

- Pizza and hamburgers are a big no-no. Not only are they high in bad fat content, they are highly caloric and can cause you to overeat

- Eat lots of fish to increase your levels of Omega 3 fatty acids

- Chicken breasts are good for you as well

- Allow yourself one cheat day a week where you can indulge in something you've been craving. Just don't overdo it on your cheat days or you can undo all you've accomplished.

- Limit the amount of fruit you eat. While fruit is healthy, it can have a detrimental effect on your workout.

- Protein and complex carbohydrates are very important

- Instead of eating three large meals a day, eat six smaller ones

- Don't skip meals

- Vegetables are always a good choice at mealtime

- When eating out, choose foods wisely.

- Avoid most fast food restaurants or opt for healthy choices – remember no burgers!

- The body is very adaptable to change. At first, you may have problems getting used to your new diet. But once you get used to eating right, you'll find yourself not even craving the foods you used to eat.

In case you're a little confused over what and how to eat, consider the following sample meal plans in the next chapter as a way of structuring your meals and staying on track.

Chapter 4: Meal Plans: Print Out

Choosing the right way to eat to build muscle can be a little overwhelming. But once you start eating the way you need to, it will become second nature to you.

Following is a list of good foods for you to eat in each of the categories you need to concentrate on:

<u>Proteins</u>

White meat chicken or turkey

Canned tuna

Canned salmon

Fresh Fish

Shellfish

Eggs

Tofu

Soy

Red meat like steak or roast

<u>Complex Carbohydrates</u>

Oatmeal

Potatoes

Yams, Sweet potatoes, Acorn squash

Rice

Legumes

Corn

<u>Vegetables</u>

All water based types.

Lettuce, Cabbage, Spinach

Asparagus

Bok Choy, Leeks

Tomatoes

Celery

Onions

Green Beans

Broccoli, Cauliflower, Radish

Zucchini Squash

Mushrooms

Carrots

Peas

<u>Fruit</u>

1 Apple

1 Orange

1/2 Grapefruit

3 Small Apricots

1 Banana

1/4 Melon

1-Cup Berries, Grapes

1 mango, small papaya

<u>Dairy</u>

1 yogurt

1-Cup low fat cottage cheese

1-Cup non-fat milk (I use vanilla soy milk instead!)

1/2 Cup non or low fat cheese

Wheat Products

2 slices whole wheat bread

1 bagel

2-Cups pasta

Whole wheat tortillas

Snack Foods

Rice cakes

Non-wheat cereals

Plain popcorn

Raw Vegetables

Nuts

Dried Fruit

A good diet is well-rounded and contains some of each of the food groups. You should also include a supplement in your diet which we will get to in a later section.

As we've said, you should be eating 5 or 6 smaller meals every day instead of three large ones. Space your meals about 2 to 2 ½ hours apart.

Sample Meal Plans

Try out a few of these meal plans to start out with.

DAY 1

Meal 1

Vegetable omelet (3 egg whites, 1 whole egg, 1 cup veggies)

You can also add some chicken or lean beef if you want.

Meal 2

One cup yogurt or a protein shake

Meal 3

6 oz Chicken

Small raw vegetable salad

1 bagel

Meal 4

1 piece fruit

3-4 oz Chicken

Meal 5

6 oz fish

1 - Cup grilled veggies

1 - Cup brown rice

DAY 2

Meal 1

3 packs instant oatmeal

1 banana

1 cup of yogurt

1 cup of cottage cheese

Meal 2

Protein shake

1 large baked potato

Meal 3

8 ounces chicken breast

2 cups pasta

1 apple

1 cup yogurt

Meal 4

1 can of tuna

1 – 2 cups broccoli

Meal 5

Protein shake

1 cup brown rice

Meal 6

8 ounces broiled fish

1 cup veggies

2 cups rice

DAY 3

Meal 1

Breakfast burrito (3 egg whites, 1 whole egg scrambled, 1 cup onion/green pepper mix, salsa)

1 cup cottage cheese

1 cup berries

Meal 2

Protein shake

1 cup raw veggies

Meal 3

Salmon burger on whole wheat bun (canned salmon, 1 egg white, onions cooked in a non-stick fry pan)

1 large potato cut into strips, brushed with olive oil, and baked in oven until crispy

1 garden salad drizzled with olive oil and red wine vinegar

Meal 4

Protein shake

1 cup yogurt

Meal 5

8 ounces chicken breast, cut into chunks, fried in olive oil and seasoned with oregano, garlic salt, and basil

1 cup cooked tomatoes

2 cups pasta

1 cup broccoli/cauliflower mix

Meal 6

Protein shake

1 cup melon

1 cup yogurt

It's a good idea to plan ahead and pre-cook your meals. Keep vegetables cut up in the refrigerator so you don't have to work too hard at mealtime.

There's really no need to measure carefully for the portions suggested. This isn't an exact science! Eyeball your portions and consider the following chart:

Portion	Portion Size
1 oz. meat	Matchbox
3 oz. meat	Deck of cards
8 oz. meat	Thin paperback book
3 oz. fish	Checkbook
1 oz. cheese	Four dice

1 med. potato	Computer mouse
2 tbsp. peanut butter	Ping pong ball
1 cup pasta	Tennis ball
1 bagel	Hockey puck

Recipes are always good to have on hand, so here's a few to try on for size.

Cooking For Mass

You don't have to be a gourmet chef to cook nutritional meals that can complement your body-building program.

Cooking can be a great way to gain control of your eating and pick what you put into your foods like salt and fat. Meals can be as simple or as complicated as you like. Here are a few recipes to get you started.

Cereal Casserole

Your favorite cereal

Skim milk

Honey

1 cup yogurt

Fill half the bowl with cereal. Add milk until it reaches the top of the cereal. Add yogurt. Top with more cereal. Add more milk. Drizzle with honey.

Protein Pancakes

1 cup of Oatmeal

11 egg whites

1 whole egg

1 packet of sugar free Jello any flavor

Stir all ingredients together in a mixing bowl. Drizzle onto hot non-stick fry pan.

Tuna or Salmon Patties

1 can tuna or salmon

1 onion

1 tablespoon of salt

1 teaspoon of pepper

1 teaspoon of parsley

1 whole egg

3 medium potatoes, boiled and mashed

Mix potatoes, tuna, onions, salt, pepper and parsley. Shape into patties. Fry in olive oil until brown and heated on both sides.

Spicy Chicken Ole

8 ounces chicken breast cut into chunks

1 can diced tomatoes or 2 medium fresh tomatoes diced

1 can spicy chili hot beans

1 medium onion chopped

Sauté chicken breast and onions in some olive oil in a frying pan. Stir in tomatoes and chili beans. Cook uncovered for ten minutes. Sprinkle with low-fat shredded Cheddar cheese.

Lightning Fast Fajitas

1 lb. flank steak cut in strips or small pieces

1 large green pepper, cut in strips

1 red pepper, cut in strips

1 medium yellow onion, cut in strips

3 cloves pressed garlic

1 tsp chili powder

Lemon juice

Fresh ground pepper to taste

Sauté garlic in a bit of lemon juice for 1 minute in large wok or skillet. Add beef and chili powder and cook until beef is cooked near to the temperature you desire. Add peppers and onions and cook until vegetables are mostly soft, raising the heat for a short time if you like the vegetables slightly charred. Spoon into whole wheat tortillas. Top with salsa or fat-free sour cream if desired.

Chicken Cacciatore

2 lbs boneless skinless chicken breast

1 28 oz can crushed tomato

1 chopped onion

1 chopped green pepper

3 pressed garlic cloves

1 tsp. thyme

1 tsp. salt

1 tsp. oregano

1 tbsp. parsley

Dash of pepper

Cooking spray

Spray pan with cooking spray and heat. Brown chicken and set aside. Add chopped onion, green pepper and garlic. Cook until the onion is tender; about 5 minutes. Add crushed tomatoes, parsley, oregano, thyme, salt and pepper. Cook over low for 15 minutes; stirring occasionally. Add browned chicken, cover and cook on low for 45 minutes. Uncover and cook an additional 15 minutes. Serve. Top on whole wheat pasta or brown rice if desired.

Pan Broiled Fish

1 lb. Fish filets

One 14 oz. Can diced tomatoes w/ basil, garlic & oregano

Arrange fish filets in a single layer in skillet. Cover with tomatoes and liquid. Cover and cook over medium heat for 10-20 minutes, or until the fish easily flakes with a fork. Serve plain or over brown rice.

Broiled Fish Dijon

6 fish filets

1 lbs small zucchini, cut lengthwise into halves

1 cup lemon juice

2 tbsp. low-calorie Dijon mustard

1 clove garlic, minced or pressed

2 tbsp. drained capers

Paprika to taste

Rinse fish and pat dry. In a separate bowl, stir together mustard and garlic. Arrange fish and zucchini in a single layer in a large pan. Drizzle with lemon juice. Broil on top rack for 5 minutes. Turn fish over, spread with mustard/garlic mixture. Continue to broil for 5 minutes or until zucchini is lightly browned and fish is cooked. Sprinkle with paprika and capers. Serve. 6 servings

Stuffed Chicken Breasts

1 chopped onion

1 pkg. frozen spinach, thawed and dried

1 egg lightly beaten

8 oz. low fat ricotta cheese

Salt & pepper to taste

4 boneless, skinless chicken breasts, slice in half and flattened

Combine the onion, spinach, egg, and cheese mixture in a bowl. Put a dollop of the mixture into each chicken breast. Tie the chicken breasts together with butchers twine, or put toothpicks through them. Bake at 350 degrees for 30-35 minutes. Optional: Garnish with lemon slices.

Ground Turkey Breast Sauce

1 lb. ground turkey or beef

1 chopped onion

1 cup chopped portabella mushrooms

1 tsp allspice

1 tsp red pepper flakes

Salt & pepper to taste

1 jar spaghetti sauce

Brown the meat with the red pepper flakes. Add the chopped onion and mushrooms. Put the all spice, salt and pepper in. Pour the spaghetti sauce in. Serve over your favorite type of noodle.

Lemon Pepper Tuna

1 can tuna

Lemon Pepper Seasoning

Spray a fry pan with no calorie non-stick cooking spray. Add tuna and sprinkle with seasoning. Cook tuna to desired doneness. Eat plain or on a bed of pasta. This is also good cold.

Worcestershire Tuna

1 can tuna

Worcestershire Sauce

No-Fat or Low-Fat Cheese (optional)

Spray a fry pan with no calorie non-stick cooking spray. Add tuna with an amount of Worcestershire Sauce that you like. Cook to desired texture. Add cheese if you like and let it melt after turning the burner off. You can eat this on some whole-wheat bread, plain, or over some brown rice.

Chicken, Rice & Beans

Cooked Shredded Chicken Breast

1 cup cooked brown rice

1 can red beans

2 tbsp. barbeque sauce

In large bowl or Tupperware, combine rice, beans, and chicken. Add barbeque sauce and stir together until well-coated.

Egg Salad Sandwich

3-4 boiled egg whites (may keep 1-2 yolks)

2 tbsp. low fat mayonnaise

1 tbsp. yellow mustard

Ground black pepper

2 slices 100% whole wheat bread

Shredded lettuce or spinach leaves

1 can tuna (optional for more protein, or just use more egg whites.

Chop egg whites and add to medium bowl. Add mayo, mustard, black pepper, and tuna. Mix well and spread over bread. Top with lettuce or spinach leaves and second slice of bread.

Tuna Casserole

3-4 cups cooked pasta

1-2 cans tuna (drained)

1 cup low fat cottage cheese (drained)

1 cup shredded low fat cheddar cheese

2 tbsp. low fat mayo

Ground black pepper

1 cup canned peas (rinsed & drained)

In medium bowl, combine all ingredients and stir until well-mixed. Microwave for approximately 1 minute when ready to serve.

Fiery Chicken Deluxe

8 oz chicken breast

Tabasco sauce (or other favorite hot sauce)

2 tsp cayenne pepper

2 tsp crushed, dried jalapeno peppers

2 pinch of salt

1 tbsp Cajun rub/spices

1 cup of frozen green beans

5 oz red potatoes

Combine the hot sauce, cayenne pepper, salt with chicken in a container and really roll the chicken breast around in the mix, then let it sit in the refrigerator for 3 - 10 hours (the longer, the juicier it will be).This works best with a Foreman-style grill. Pre-heat, then slap the chicken on and cook for 7 minutes

While the chicken is cooking, stab the red potatoes and cook in the microwave for 4 ½ minutes or until soft in the middle.Take the potatoes out, and put the green beans in for 2 - 3 minutes.Smash the potatoes and sprinkle on a pinch of salt and the crushed jalapeno peppers.Sprinkle the other pinch of salt on the green beans

Grilled Chicken Asparagus Rolls

1 chicken breast

2 asparagus sticks

2 slices of low fat turkey bacon

1 tsp Dijon mustard

1 tbsp honey

Salt and pepper to taste

Once the chicken breast is washed trim the fat from it. Cut chicken into two to four thin slices, depending on how thick you would like your roll to be. Put chicken slices in the container; add the salt and pepper, mustard and honey. Let it marinate for 25 minutes. Give the asparagus a quick wash. Snap off tough ends of asparagus and remove scales with vegetable peeler. Place one slice of turkey bacon on each slice of chicken breast. Place one asparagus stick on the top and start rolling it.

Once the roll is ready, use a couple of wooden picks to secure the turkey bacon - ensure the picks are placed in such a way the chicken meat maintains its shape around the roll. You can grill rolls than for seven minutes on the electric grill at 375 degrees, or bake them for 25 minutes at 375 degrees.

Three Minute Scallops

1 cup dry white wine

2 cloves garlic, minced

1 tsp. Dried parsley

Juice of 1 lemon

1 lb. Fresh bay scallops, rinsed and patted dry.

Heat wine in a medium skillet over medium heat. Add garlic and sauté 1 minute. Add parsley and lemon juice. Cover and cook 1 minute. Add scallops and cook 1 minute or until scallops turn from translucent to opaque. Makes 2-3 servings

Garlic Roasted Vegetables

6 carrots, peeled and quartered

6 parsnips, peeled and quartered

6 shallots, peeled and halved

2 medium onions, peeled and cut into 6-8 wedges

1 large garlic bulb, broken into cloves and peeled

1 tbsp. dried rosemary, or 3 tbsp. fresh, chopped

1 tbsp. dried thyme, or 3 tbsp. fresh

4 tbsp. olive oil

In the Oven: Preheat oven to 400 F. Combine all the vegetables in roasting pan, drizzle with oil and stir to coat. Roast for about 1 hour 20 minutes or until tender. Salt and pepper to taste.

On the Grill: Turn barbeque to medium. Combine all the vegetables into a tinfoil bag, drizzle with olive oil and stir to coat. Roast for about 30 minutes or until tender. Salt and pepper to taste. Great with meat, chicken and fish.

Chicken Salad Roll-ups

1 lb. boneless, skinless chicken, cooked

2 tbsp. sunflower seeds

2 tbsp. dried fruit bits

1/8 cup celery, diced

1/3 cup nonfat yogurt

Fresh Leaf Lettuce

Dice chicken, and place in mixing bowl. Combine with sunflower seeds, fruit bits, celery, and yogurt. Spread a little chicken mixture on lettuce leaf and roll up tightly. Repeat until mixture is used up. Serve immediately, or wrap roll-ups in plastic wrap for later use. Makes two servings

Fish in Foil

1 lb. halibut, cut in two pieces

1 tomato, chopped

1 green onion, chopped

4 small zucchini, julienne

1 carrot, julienne

1 cup dry white wine

1 tsp. each fresh dill and parsley

Dash of freshly ground pepper

Preheat oven to 400 degrees. Cut two 12 in. square pieces of foil. Place a piece of fish on each square of foil. Top each piece of fish with tomato, green onion, zucchini, and carrot. Sprinkle each with wine, herbs, and pepper. Fold foil edges together, sealing with a pleat. Bake for 15 minutes. Makes two servings

Muscle Building Shake

1 cup ice cubes

1 cup egg whites

1 cup vanilla soy milk

1 cup frozen strawberries

1 banana

1 cup cranberry juice

Put all ingredients in a blender and blend on high for 30 seconds. Drink.

Workout Energy Salad

1 cup lettuce, torn into bite-sized pieces

1/3 cup spinach, torn into bite-sized pieces

1/3 cucumber, peeled and sliced

1/3 tomato, sliced

1 cup sprouts

1/3 cup shredded carrots

1/3 cup sliced mushrooms

1/3 avocado, cubed

1 tbsp raw sunflower seeds

1 tbsp olive oil

2 tsp lemon juice

Dash each of thyme, parsley, basil

In a medium-sized salad bowl, combine lettuce, spinach, cucumber, tomato, sprouts, carrots, mushrooms, avocado, and sunflower seeds. In a screw-top jar, mix olive oil with lemon juice and herbs. Shake vigorously, and pour over salad.

Muscle Density Broccoli Salad

1 pound cooked steak, cut in strips

1 cup broccoli, cooked and chopped

1 cup green beans, cooked and cut

1 stalk celery, sliced

1 cup mushrooms, sliced

1 green onion, sliced

1 tbsp red wine vinegar

1 tbsp lemon juice

1 cup nonfat yogurt

1 tsp mustard

1 tsp ground pepper

1 head of lettuce

1 tomato, sliced

Fresh parsley

In large salad bowl, combine steak, broccoli, green beans, celery, mushrooms, and onion. In a screw-top jar, combine the vinegar, lemon juice, yogurt, mustard, and pepper, and shake until thoroughly mixed for the salad dressing. Arrange salad on a bed of lettuce leaves. Garnish with tomato slices and parsley

Protein Smoothie

1 cup fat free milk

1 cup fat free vanilla yogurt

1/3 cup frozen blueberries

1 cup frozen cherries

1 cup Egg Beaters

1 Banana

Toss all of the ingredients into a blender and blend until smooth.

Nutrition is very important when you are trying to build up muscle mass. You don't necessarily have to be dieting, but you do have to be conscious about what you are putting into your body so that you can maximize your workouts.

Another huge thing you have to be aware of in your body building program is sleep.

Chapter 5: Rested Performance

Sleep is one of your most valuable tools for growth that you can have in your body building arsenal. Muscle adaptation and growth often occurs at night. During the suspended state of animation you are in, your body is doing exactly what you have been asking it to do during your workouts – build muscle.

Lack of sleep can have an intoxicating effect on your body. According to the Journal of Applied Sports Science, being awake for 24 hours has the same physical effect as a blood alcohol content of 0.096, which is above the legal driving limit in most states.

Working out in this state has its obvious downside. For starters, your lack of muscular coordination places you at a much higher risk for injury. Just as you'd never head to the gym after drinking a few beers at your local tavern, you should never work out after not sleeping the night before. You're better off waiting until the next day when your body has been given proper rest.

What are the best practices when it comes to getting enough sleep? Here are some pointers:

Don't exercise before bedtime. Body temperature has a huge effect on our ability to fall asleep. As your body temperature lowers, you start to feel sleepy.

If you work up a sweat before trying to sleep, you will have difficulty falling asleep and it could take your body several hours to cool down enough so that you can drift off.

Try having a light snack before bedtime. Some people disagree with this theory, but if you go to bed on an empty stomach, it can distract from your ability to fall asleep. Make sure this snack is light, though.

Get at least eight hours of quality sleep per night. This will insure that you get the rest and recovery that your body needs to be able to function effectively during the day. Keep your bedroom dark and cool. Try having some white noise in the room like a fan running.

Don't drink a lot of fluids before sleep, especially tea or coffee. Not only will the caffeine keep you awake, but you'll have to use the bathroom more often as well which will disturb your sleep.

Establish both a regular sleep cycle as well as a pre-sleep routine. This will help you signal your body that it's time to think about resting. While your body is sleeping, your body's synthesis of protein increases. This is what makes you grow. Your body can recover and repair any damage you did during the day while you are at rest.

A majority of growth hormones are also released when the body is in the sleep state. Growth hormones are very important in increasing muscle mass. During a workout, growth hormones are also released, but the majority of this happens while the body is at rest. Just as sleep will give you more energy, it is also vital in helping your body recover and ultimately grow like you want it to.

As we said before, you will want to take supplements when you really want to grow your body. They can be confusing, though.

Chapter 6: The Truth About Supplements

There are literally hundreds of supplements on the market targeted at body builders and meant to increase your body size. They are designed to maximize the body's natural abilities and help you get the body mass you want.

How do you know which supplement is right for you?

Creatine

Creatine is the most popular and commonly used sports supplement available today. There are numerous studies backed by anecdotal evidence that support the efficacy of creatine supplementation.

For the majority of the population, including both elite athletes and untrained individuals, creatine supplementation increases fat free mass and improves anaerobic and possibly aerobic performance.

Creatine is a natural constituent of meat, mainly found in red meat. Creatine is manufactured naturally in the body from the amino acids glycine, arginine, and methionine. This process takes place in the kidneys, liver, and pancreas.

Approximately 40% of the body's creatine stores are free creatine (Cr), while the remaining 60% is stored in form of creatine phosphate (CP).

The typical male adult processes 2 grams of creatine per day, and replaces that amount through dietary intake and fabrication within the body.

Creatine is used for the resynthesis of ATP. ATP, or adenosine triphosphate, is the "power" that drives muscular energetics.

When a muscle is required to contract, the bonds in the ATP molecule are split, yielding ADP (adenosine-diphosphate). The energy released by breaking this bond powers the contraction of the muscle.

When ATP is depleted within the cell, the cell can no longer contract. There are several methods by which the body rebuilds ATP.

The fastest method, without oxygen, is through CP. Creatine phosphate is "split" to yield the phosphate portion of the molecule.

This phosphate portion bonds to the ADP, turning it back to ATP. Once CP stores within the cell are depleted, the body must use other methods to replenish ATP.

Supplementation with creatine increases Cr and CP within the muscle, allowing further capacity to regenerate ATP.

In other words, the creatine enhances the ability of the muscle to maintain power output during brief periods of high-intensity exercise.

The periods are brief because the ability of a cell to store CP is limited, therefore the body will quickly move to other methods of replenishing ATP.

There are two way to decide what dosage of creatine you should take. In the "loading phase" which is where you begin adding creatine to your diet, the dosage is 20 grams a day for five to seven days. After that, it's recommended that you stick to 5 grams per day.

You can also calculate creatine dosage according to body weight and mass. Follow along closely, this could get confusing! Not really, though.

Experts say in the "loading phase", you should be consuming .3 grams of creatine per kilogram of body weight. So if you weight 200 pounds, the formula would look like this:

1 lb divided by 2.2 kg multiplied by .3 = 27 grams of creatine per day

After the loading phase, your weight is multiplied by .03, so you would require 2.7 grams in the maintenance phase.

Essentially, creatine can create muscle fullness as well as create an environment within your body that is conducive to muscle growth. It can also delay fatigue during repeated workouts. However, you must use your creatine regularly instead of sporadically for it to be effective.

Creatine is also thought to increase the body's aerobic abilities. One study showed that using creatine supplements help to reduce the oxygen cost of activity so less strain is placed on the cardiovascular system while performing aerobic activity. This is a huge advantage for the body builder as this means you will be able to work harder and longer losing fat and building up muscle.

Creatine is safe for most everyone to take with the exception of people with renal issues. Doctors are even beginning to endorse creatine which is generally unheard of with supplements.

Many people like to take their creatine in a shake as it most often comes in the form of powder. You can mix the creatine powder with some skim or soy milk and even add some fresh fruit for flavor.

It is generally a good idea to have your creatine after you workout so that the glycogen in your body is replenished and recovery can be enhanced.

Glutamine

Another popular supplement among body builders is glutamine. Glutamine is a non-essential amino acid that is produced naturally by the body. Sixty percent of glutamine is found in the skeletal muscles. The remainder is in the lung, liver, brain, and stomach tissues. Over 60% of our amino acids come in the form of glutamine. Under normal conditions, our body can produce more than enough. However, during times of stress, glutamine reserves are depleted and must be replenished through supplementation. This includes stress that the body is under during periods of exercise. If you have too little glutamine in your system, it can result in muscle loss. This amino acid is essential to muscle building because it helps nitrogen in the body move around to where it needs to be. You have to have a positive nitrogen balance in order to gain muscle mass.

Creatine is also thought to prevent sickness, promote healing, prevent sore muscles, and speed up growth hormone production. The typical American diet provides 3.5 to 7 grams of glutamine daily which is found in animal and plant proteins. Many people are choosing to supplement daily due to the long growing list of benefits. Research shows levels of supplementation from 2 to 40 grams daily. Two to three grams has been found to help symptoms of queasiness. This two to three gram dosage used post workout builds protein, repairs and builds muscle and can induce levels of growth hormone found in the body.

If you want to build a ripped body, you'll need both creatine and glutamine alike. Again, it usually comes in powder form, so you'll want to take it with milk or in a shake.

Protein

The importance of protein to a body builder is a no-brainer. It is the single most important nutrient in a body-building regimen.

Protein is what makes up and maintains most of the stuff in our bodies. Protein has been shown to have the best effects on the body when combined with carbohydrates.

Much of your protein will come from your diet, but if you really want to grow your body mass, increasing protein through weight gainers or protein powders is necessary. Of course, you'll need to be careful not to overdo it and monitor the amount of protein you are consuming.

The best type of protein supplement on the market is whey protein because it is the highest yield. Whey is the best investment because of its capacity as a post-workout recovery supplement.

This is a critical time after severe physical stress when the cells will act like a sponge and take in almost anything. The extreme hunger of the cells and the fast-acting properties of whey will make sure you use the best window for recovery to the fullest. If not, the body will hunt the stored reserves of nutrients and when on a diet for example that will cause them to rob other muscle-tissue of glutamine.

So whey is the best protein, especially on a diet. It also supplies the most amino acids that bodybuilders use. Its unfortunate high cost however makes me advise you to use it sparingly. Whey protein is the only choice when on a diet however. When on low-carb diets whey can function as an alternate source of energy, sparing hard-earned muscle protein and glutamine stores within the body.

As with creatine, the best time to take your protein supplement is post-workout. As we said before, it's good to combine your protein with some form of carbohydrate for maximum results. Combine the powder with some eggs, low-fat milk, ice cream, and olive oil. You can also add in some fruit for flavor.

Nitric Oxide

Another powerful supplement you can take as part of your body building program is nitric oxide. Many body builders take nitric oxide for a variety of reasons.

Nitric Oxide, a key molecule manufactured by the body, causes vasodilation [an expansion of the internal diameter of blood vessels], which in turn leads to increased blood flow, oxygen transport, delivery of nutrients to skeletal muscle and a reduction in blood pressure.

Nitric oxide promotes extended ability to life weights. It also signals muscle growth, speeds recovery, and increases strength along with stamina. This element also increases energy levels and some people even feel that it promotes a better sex life!

During a workout, when a muscle contracts and blood vessels dilate, Nitric Oxide is present for a brief moment. The release of nitric oxide creates surges of blood flow, which is the muscle pump we are familiar with. Unfortunately this pump is only temporary, and will dissipate shortly after you complete your workout.

It often comes in pill form, and should be taken in the manufacturer's recommended dosage. Nitric oxide also comes in powder form as well, so you can take it in a shake just like with other powdered supplements.

Steroids and Growth Hormones

We're not going to spend a lot of time on these types of supplements because they are certainly not recommended, but they are used by body builders all over the world. Both of these substances are highly controversial, and in many places, they are illegal.

Steroids and growth hormones stimulate muscle growth often quite quickly which is why they are so popular among body builders. They also enhance performance making a person stronger and extending their stamina.

Steroid use is generally not condoned in the sports world and constant testing is done of the athletes to see if they are getting an unfair advantage by using steroids or growth hormones.

Steroids do have some advantages. They are used in treating a variety of health problems including AIDS, cancer, and other serious diseases. They help the body fight the ill effects of these diseases and promote healing.

However, steroids have some serious health implications when taken for reasons other than therapeutic. They can cause serious liver damage and even lead to liver failure. Steroids increase testosterone production which can lead to overly aggressive behavior, a decrease in libido, and low sperm count.

The reason many body builders use steroids is because they increase water retention in the muscles which leads to an anabolic state. However, this increase in fluid retention makes the heart work harder which can increase blood pressure and even bring on a heart attack.

All steroids eventually change to estrogen which causes feminization in men. That causes an enlargement of the breasts along with an increase in fatty deposits.

Growth hormones stimulate the elements in the body that make muscles grow. They are naturally produced by the body, but many body builders take them to basically tell their muscles to get bigger. They can be dangerous, though, as well.

You can get huge, ripped muscles without having to resort to using illegal substances like steroids or artificial growth hormones. They can make you bigger quicker, but the disadvantages far outweigh the advantages you are taking by introducing these substances into your body.

Body building has long been thought of as a man's sport, but more and more women are getting interested in it as well.

Chapter 7: Body Building For Women

Some women have never considered bodybuilding as a sport because they are simply concerned that if they weight train, they will end up losing their feminine figure, and instead appear big, bulky and masculine.

Nothing could be further from the truth.

Women cannot naturally produce the amount of testosterone that men do, so it is impossible for women to increase their muscle size in the same ways that men do just by picking up a weight or two. Without artificial substances, women won't be able to get the same bulk as men do.

However, many of the same workout advice that we give to men apply to women as well: eat 5-6 small meals per day, drink plenty of water, and get lots of rest. The workouts are the same as well although some women may want to limit their reps initially until their strength is built up.

Many women struggle with excess fat and flabby muscle tone on their thighs and in their buttocks. Because women are naturally curvier than men, working these areas makes for a very flattering figure.

To work these areas, you will want to do a lot of dumbbell squats, leg curls, standing calf raises, and leg presses. Add some lunges as well as dumbbell squat dead lifts as well for maximum effectiveness. You may want to invest in an exercise ball so that you can work your abs and make them tight and defined.

Change your workout every time you perform it and focus on one or two body parts each day you train. By doing this, you are not over-exerting muscles without giving them time to heal.

Recovery is very important to the body's muscles, so give them the time they need to heal and grow. Many women live their lives by the numbers that they read on a scale. When you are bodybuilding for fitness, this is an absolute mistake. Don't concentrate on what the scale says you weigh, focus on your size and tone.

This can be calculated in the form of inches or body fat percentage. You will probably not see a huge weight loss on the scale, but you should see an improvement in your overall body's look after a period of time.

Here are some areas that women should really focus on in their body building routine:

Upper Back – Use pull-ups to build the muscles in your upper back which will accentuate your shoulders and make your waist look smaller.

Side Deltoids – Side laterals and overhead laterals will help tone these muscles making your shoulders more defined and, again, your waist look smaller.

Hips and Waist – These areas are mostly chiseled through diet by teaching the body to re-distribute body fat.

It is the finishing signature to the rest of your body and will make your overall appearance look much more pleasant.

Quads – The front muscles in your upper thighs need to be worked so that they are toned and defined. Doing lots of squats will help in this area and will complete your overall look. After all, what woman doesn't want to have some killer legs!

Women are used to dieting and depriving themselves of food. When you are body building, however, the reality is that you need to actually eat more. The key lies in the foods that you eat. Eat the right foods, and they will work for you instead of against you!

As a woman, you need to remember that you will not be able to build your muscle like men do; however, your approach toward body building will be much the same.

Chapter 8: A Note About Competitions

As you get more and more into the sport of body building, you may want to consider showing off your hard work by entering into a body building competition.

There are many local gyms that hold contests as well as national competitions that are held on an annual basis. Before you actually enter a body building competition, you really need to know what they're all about in the first place.

Take the time to attend a competition before entering and pay close attention to the techniques the exhibitors use and ask questions about what the judges are looking for.

Do not enter a body building contest just because you've lost a bunch of weight. These contests are about great physiques with toned muscles – not about people who've lost body fat.

Your muscles must be well-defined and toned ready for display. Be realistic about your chances the first time out. While it is possible to realize a "Cinderella" story finish, it's not really probable when you consider that some of the other entrants are very experienced. Tell yourself that you'll be happy with not being cut from the lineup or taking fifth place, for example, which is a realistic goal for many beginners.

Once you've decided on a competition, you need to start planning well ahead of time to become fully prepared for contest day. You need to concentrate on any problem areas you have and work them hard. Keep up with your regular routine, so the muscles that are already toned don't lose their definition.

Think about what you will wearing during the contest and what songs you will want played while you are posing. You will also want to start thinking about your posing routine. We'll interject a quick note about suits here since it's not really that complicated choosing what you're going to wear.

You have worked very hard on your body, and in a contest, you will want to show off as much of it as possible. Pick a suit in a color that is complementary and one that is as skimpy as you are comfortable with.

Just don't over-do it – it's not about who shows the most skin but who shows the best muscles.

With music, you will want to choose songs that will activate and excite the crowd. Judges will respond better to you if you have a lot of clapping and cheering going on for you.

Your posing style will be dictated by the music, either elegant or aggressive depending on your selection. Your style of music is important. Your mood, the mood of the audience and the judges will be set moment by moment, heavily balance by the competitor's choices of music.

Clearly defined space in the music for major poses is usually extremely important. Some routines flow perfectly and gracefully through music without accentuating beats, but you can be confident that only a few competitors in a hundred can successfully achieve the beauty and grace of such a performance.

If you don't have a childhood background in dance or ballet, or you don't have a nearly perfect body with matching symmetry, try to select music with a pronounced beat where you can clearly put your strongest poses.

We can't stress enough that you can have a great physique, but if you don't know how to show it off, you won't be doing any good in a contest.

Posing is so very important in competition. It gives the judges an idea of what they are looking for in a contestant, which is symmetry, muscularity, aesthetics, and proportions.

A good place to start learning about posing is to look through body building magazines to see how the models are presenting themselves.

Try out a few of these poses while looking at yourself in a full-length mirror. What works for one person may not work for you, but it just might!

Think about the beat of your music and then choose poses that go along with that beat. Start out with your most powerful pose and hold it for 3 to 5 full seconds.

Make sure that your routine flows smoothly and there is enough time in between poses for a little fun.

What muscles should you be accentuating? The easiest answer is all of them, but you will want to show off certain parts of your body specifically.

You need to know your muscles, and we hope by now you do. Here are some areas you will want to focus on:

Front Double Bicep

Arms are out to the sides with biceps flexed and the competitor is facing forward towards the judges and audience.

Front Lat Spread

Hands are located somewhere near the competitor's waistline and elbows are flared out showing the lats. The competitor is facing forward.

Side Chest

The competitor is turned so judges can see his profile. He has one calf flexed by raising his heel from the ground. Hands are clasped or wrist is grabbed with the back arm coming across the front of the torso somewhere below the pec line.

The forward arm is pulled down and back toward the competitor's rear. The chest is raised and flexed. The rib cage is usually expanded.

Side Tricep

The competitor is in the same basic position as the side chest except his arms are clasped behind him.

The forward arm is flexed straight down showing off the triceps.

The back arm is stretched across the lower back and it's hand is clasped with the forward arm's hand.

Abdominal and Thigh

The competitor is now facing forward. His arms are tucked behind his head and one leg is placed farther forward than the other and flexed. The competitor is also flexing his abdominal muscles.

Rear Double Bicep

The competitor is facing the rear of the stage away from the judges and audience.

Arms are out to the sides and biceps are flexed. One leg is back and that calf is flexed. The back muscles are also flexed.

Rear Lat Spread

The competitor is in the same basic position as the Back Double Biceps except the hands are attached at the waist and the elbows are pulled out and the lats are flared outward.

Classic "Strong Man" Body Building Pose

Typically, judges will call for the competitor's favorite most muscular pose. At this point, they have the option to hit whichever of the most muscular poses they feel make them look the best.

If you want to come up with some poses of your own, by all means do so! You know your body best of all and if there are certain muscles you really want to show off – such as your glutes – definitely do it!

When you come up with a posing routine, you should practice so that you know it like the back of your hand. If you hear your music on the radio, you should be doing your routine in your head.

Every chance you get, watch yourself going through the routine and maximizing your muscle tone so that you make an impressive performance.

Have someone take pictures or video of you and be highly critical of it. You can also have someone else look at it for you and tell you where you can improve and where you are strongest.

While you are posing, breathe normally and focus on flexing of the muscles. You want to appear cut and ripped as much as possible.

Quite a bit of time before the competition, you will want to start tanning. Tanned muscles look a lot better and more defined than non-tanned muscles.

If you don't want to risk going to a tanning bed, look at a spray-on tan the day before your competition, but be advised that these types of tanning can have an orange appearance and could detract from the image you are trying to project.

During the competition, there will be a variety of rounds during which you will compete for points.

Each contest is different, but most will have the following rounds:

Standing Relaxed Symmetry Round

During this time, the judges are looking for overall body symmetry in the competitors. They are looking for relationships between the muscle groups.

Are they all developed evenly? Within each specific group, does it flow nicely? Does the competitor have a symmetrical bone structure?

The more evenly developed the competitor is, the higher he or she will be placed.

There is no direct flexing in this round. Competitors are viewed in what is called the Standing Relaxed position.

Typically, this consists of the competitor's heels together, toes pointed out at a forty-five degree angle, and lats semi-flared.

Every competitor has their own way of standing relaxed, but in reality it is semi-flexed.

Every muscle should be tight on stage. The competitors are viewed from the front, both sides, and the rear.

Comparison or Muscularity Round

This is where the real flexing begins! Competitors are called upon to hit the Mandatory poses in this round.

The judges are comparing the level of muscular development and definition each competitor has acquired in relation to the other competitors.

Free Posing Round

The Free Posing Round is where each competitor gets to express their muscularity how they see fit. Usually, this round is accompanied by music.

If there are no restrictions on oiling, you will want to apply a thin coat of baby oil to your body.

This can enhance your muscle tone and make you appear more cut. Some avid body builders also advocate using Preparation H or some other type of hemorrhoid cream. These creams pull water out from under the skin. When a body builder has excess water in the skin, he or she will look smooth and undefined.

Many bodybuilders who have used creatine supplements during their workout routine will lay off about four to six weeks before the competition. Then, three to five days before, they load up again just like when they first started which will make them look fuller.

On the day before and the day of the competition, do a carb load. Don't overdo it or you will look smooth, but try having 200 grams the day before and 300 the day of. Know your body and know what makes it look good and what doesn't.

You should also mentally prepare for competing. Have your mind set on your goal as to why you wanted to enter a competition in the first place. Visualize yourself up on the stage hitting your poses and imagine the audience cheering you on. Mental preparation can be just as important as physically preparing when in comes to a successful body building competition showing.

You can find some great support and guidance in a variety of places.

Conclusion

Many people start out body building in an attempt to lose weight. That's a great way to start. But then, they start learning about what their body is doing during a workout and what is capable of when pushed.

After that door is opened, it's like Pandora's box, very difficult to close and you'll find yourself becoming addicted to the burn, the rush and the adrenaline as your body transforms into a lean, mean ripped machine J

Weight training and overall body building does require hard work and a lot of dedication, but if you commit to your overall goals, when you are finally able to look at yourself in the mirror and like what you see, the end result will be well worth any sacrifice you have made along the way.

Get started right away. You don't have to wait any longer. Your dream body is more than a possibility – it's now, finally, a reality.

To your new life!